ALSO BY MICHAEL DICKMAN

Poetry

The End of the West

Flies

Green Migraine

Plays

50 American Plays

(with Matthew Dickman)

DAYS & DAYS

Michael Dickman

POEMS

DAYS & DAYS

Alfred A. Knopf *New York* 2019

THIS IS A BORZOI BOOK
PUBLISHED BY ALFRED A. KNOPF

www.aaknopf.com

Knopf, Borzoi Books, and the colophon are registered trademarks of Penguin Random House LLC.

Library of Congress Cataloging-in-Publication Data
Names: Dickman, Michael, [date] author.
Title: Days & days : poems / by Michael Dickman.
Other titles: Days and days
Description: First edition. | New York : Alfred A. Knopf, 2019.
Identifiers: LCCN 2018029976 (print) | LCCN 2018030525 (ebook) |
ISBN 9780525655480 (ebook) | ISBN 9780525655473 (hardcover)
Classification: LCC PS3604.I299 (ebook) | LCC PS3604.I299
A6 2019 (print) | DDC 811/.6—dc23
LC record available at https://lccn.loc.gov/2018029976

Jacket image: Swallowtail Butterfly by arlindo71/E+/Getty Images
Jacket design by Olivia Croom

Manufactured in the United States of America

First Edition

for

MAVIS

CONTENTS

DAYS & DAYS

Butterfly Days

Out-of-focus icing on a cake no one can see or eat

a Princess cake or a Strawberry

window cake

One tree is sugar
One tree is completely covered

The shrubs shake it off
this afternoon
nervous all morning & then
something else

more difficult to describe

a dustup
around a brown & orange aura
or Lorca's flowers

A swallowtail lands a front foot impossible to 360 shuvit in the gloxinia
on the first try

Lorca's flowers!

Radio silence cuts the clover
or a brand-new podcast
broadcasts everything
around us

Fritillaries sigh in hi-fi

If I had a microwave
I could spend more time
in the backyard

Drink
the same cup of coffee
the same backyard

Nectaring on a trellis if I had a trellis

Fat pinks
nose open every
piece of grass

You can't do that in a microwave

Summer noise shoved through a cassette deck in the underleaf & still
those butterflies are not the Circle Jerks

High on Molly
into ammonia fertilizer
or whatever

is there beneath the sink

or the smallest movement ripples through leaves

One day is static
One day is completely gone

The swimming pool is the lawn
blue-green & no
diving board

I have a guest pass
a white sound
when I move my hands
above my head

Dusted before 10 a.m.

Butterflies are all bring your friends

Butterflies are all chlorine will highlight your summer hair but don't
drink it whatever you do or don't do

Neon tubing smolders in the fennel
or some other lightbulbs
you're not supposed to touch
with your fingers

Brite White
Peach Pink &
Rose

Look what I brought you
It's all just graffiti

I want to write your name in aerosol along the pinnule of a fiddlehead

All-city in the air

Antennas discharge in the yard & won't be replaced

A cloud moves
the colors around a
jittery ball

That's not
just green
it's

StreetGlow green

Midges scribble
in the real summer grass
or white fiberglass
made out of laundry detergent Saran wraps
the sunflowers

One butterfly is coming right back
One butterfly is no comply

They don't die

They stay above the day in a scrum

Glass wool
pulled apart & sprinkled
over the yard
flicks the outer margins

If you're so terrified of everything why don't you just stay inside?

Swallowtails drink glucose
through a straw

Everyone is going to calm down

Everyone is going to calm down

All-City

From end to end
bus stops wait for anyone
& blue jays pick
at clouds

Your name here your name there

A marble
jumps a bell & spray paint
fogs the city planners

Black-blond heavy metal bees cut right through
& stop on a dime

Every now & then a sucker butterfly gets courageous

Azaleas bloom between benches

That blue jay
fades the ferns & backtracks
from the start of day
until now

You can spend your whole life staring into John Clare's underwear &
still those enclosures can't

unsign your mind

Scribble

Some sun above the day
a squiggly light that waits round or
scribbles over
a school of Radio Cabs
& bubble letters

A doe
A deer
A female deer

Traffic moves in
the leaves & then stops
to say hello

Their noses are grape Mr. Sketch

Writing
through the names of trees

Glossy
pasterns & butt-white
Nikes are a thing

King Krylon
        with removable cap they don't make that anymore is no longer
                a thing it
                      sent out green shoots & wet buds the color of
                            early spring

The Poem Said

The poem said
mow it again
A powder of clippings floats to the surface of a cool nap in a secured
  sunspot
Paper bags line up
Neighbor dogs are kind & hunt balls to death

I would go there right now
folded up in the silence of a maple tree in the front yard
A tiara
if I could get one leaf right
& sleep in air

What would we do if we had no money?
Listen to those golden cutters hustling down this very same street
What would we do my true loves?
Dogs are for later
We polish the dogs

Hotel Days

Eco-Pillows
float above the standard queen
a dream in off-white   O

You can buy these same
pillows in the lobby
poked through
with goose feathers

The noise in the hallway is not quiet noise

A towel draped over the TV & even though it's not my home I move
the furniture around

A Visa card
slides open the exit
at a cruising altitude of 30,000 feet
Air-conditioning & Xanax
are the same thing

Alive all the time

I think I'm going to be sick

Afraid of early checkout
the continental breakfast & neighbors
through the walls
or room service 24/7
afraid of room service &
Starlights

The soft whirrup-whirrup
of an ice machine the soft
whirrup-whirrup

Large foam takeout spacecraft containers overflow the garbage in
the bath

You can't call anyone from this phone can you?

Clean sheets need a haircut
Remote control
needs a haircut

The room smells of lo mein

The pool stays open until ten if you don't have a swimsuit they will
give you one it's a new poem by Frank O'Hara

Elevators
reach up inside themselves like trees
& do
their tree arms

A bird here a bird there

Employees change the welcome mat three times a day unseen

Good morning
Good afternoon
Good evening

The noise in the hallway is business

That first moment when you walk in & flop down on the bed is pure
chemical relief until it isn't

On the 100th floor
a twin pattern helicopters down
a carpet without end

High windows

On a clear day you can see whatever

Women work
from room to room
with smoke breaks & water glasses
samples wrapped
in pink plastic

I never know if I can use the bathrobes or not

Windows bolted past the first story & toilet seats tied up with paper
ribbon are safe & clean as deep freeze

The mountains here
don't allow cell service or
cigarettes

A living water repeats in the lobby

I keep the air
turned up no matter what
it makes a kind of weather

Executive leather!

From the airport to the front desk in nothing flat

A brand-new rolly suitcase kisses the carpet

Doors open by themselves
lights are on a timer you could be
anywhere & some people
like that   O

The noise in the hallway is children

Country & Western

This used to be a smoking room or this was never a smoking room &
    in some places you drive straight up to the door

A bowl of free oranges
health muffins &
who's going to pay for all this?

Polished & Blurry

I fold my clothes
out of a bag into a
drawer

You're not from around here

You're not from around here

The Poem Said

The poem said
exhale Windex between a windowsill & a hummingbird or
  the neighbor's new car
The hummingbird
that was just here & the one that disappeared are
the same hummingbird

A list of trees
& a playground riddled with kids call home
or text wings &
backpacks
Now I can do whatever I want to

A seedpod explodes above the blacktop
Light pours out on top
I coughed up Excedrin in a Corolla & felt much better
There are different kinds of light
Chirps squeaks whistles & buzzes

Sticky Side

Thinking of you today your
flowers crool
on a cop

Slapped on & forgotten

The sticky side of every conifer fern is
not a fern but still
every tiny red hop a fresh fern
wiggles & jiggles like
neoprene

We stashed the markers & the faster grasses in a pudge & called our
parents they were stars

The stars above!

The Jiffy Lube is a landmark in a crappola

Packs of boys
or ewes call from every corner
their coats answer I
wrote your name all over town
in every shade of cherry-red
lip gloss &

capped their asses for free

Fat Cap

Marcel Duchamp's rose garden
a test garden
Roses
throw up on mass transit in French
downtown where they
write writing

A small brown deer nibbles the heat off a small green leaf

His baseball cap turned backward

Hurricane style
Are you ready
on the right?

A master blaster
mama deer
will charge you if you
get too close
with a cellphone or your own kids
Better from a distance
just off the shoulder a falter
or halter top

Just in time
your ready-made silver Sharpies & real fur collar getting up on the back
of the bus

TV Days

Tinfoiled rabbit ears reach out to the stars above & love what you see
Drapes draped for the afternoon
I want to see something good
but too much can
give you a stomachache

Crickets in the lining of a suit jacket or early spring & there you are
static jumps from my programs onto the carpet
tinfoil
tinfoil
trefoil

Nobody wants to fuck anymore like rabbits still it's an option
on the other side of the cereal
One cloud
is like another inside a TV show
I don't know what's it called

Pro sports call from one channel & car lots the other clouds
cloud above the both of them
Do you think
there's weather in there?
A cold front

that can freeze your teeth followed by sunlight
laid down like 2x4's
from one channel to the next you can't smell lake water
The horizon liquefies in our laps
or not

& butters our popcorn a prime time
that knows love or not
A parterre made of fissions floral arrangements
& snacks
You used to have to get up & walk across the floor

Flick it over
from one brown moth narrating atop a white
each spasm off-kilter
in front of electric ferns Zenith
antennas ripple

not through a light switch better than rain or a brand-new
club drug
brought to you by actors
Flick it back
a commercial break is full of cats

I don't smoke
the same cigarettes
as him
What an afternoon
hot bright transmissions in a pool cool living room

not a tree anywhere
Jellyfish on the flat-screen reach out to tell us something important
from tiled grocery aisles where in between shows
hair & makeup are on a woozy
rampage

Rainbow magnetic tape connects the heart in my chest like spaghetti
Reach for something just out
of reach
Everyone looks so good or not in clothes
Teens do

or not & the living dead & ray tubes are shorter & chirp
Nature is renewed again & again
chirp
chirp
chirp

goes the night outside the picture window & the usual grass flicks on
You look just great in your new hair & renewed season
even though & so do we
It's nice to have something to look forward to
An Ativan

inside a mountain
A cloud wandering down a sidewalk
Snow asleep on the davenport
Perspectives slide around a lot
The whole family aglow in liquid crystal

Clicker has dandruff
Commercial has dandruff
A cortisone shot
bent at the elbow & we're live
A cache of sunshine dribbles out reruns of

freshly mown grass it
opens
up
every
afternoon

The Poem Said

The poem said
perennials levitate above the yard a perfect circle of multi-touch &
  mid-afternoon rainbows
They bark for treats & a scratch
soft pink paw pads
a sliding glass door

Hallucinating in the grass everything smells different
Not my dogs
but the couch does
Weird ants in the ground cover
burst into tears

Deer ferns wave from an open container
A pocketful of melatonin
If you're looking for something to do there's always the refrigerator
A stipe in the car alarm
A skirr in the kibble

Prescription Days

Every ten feet opposite the new faculty housing inside my tree-lined
mind an automatic sprinkler

It's going to be a beautiful day
& so are you

Crack the ice tray
& dandelions degloss their preschool yellow voices freeze-dried &
recently vacuumed

No thanks I don't drink
The morning is Externo light & juice

Ice in a cup
Spoon balanced on the tip of your finger

I jump for joy among powdered pastels
& hear my teeth

Everything else waits
The loops in the front yard wait where every piece of grass whispers
hold on a minute

Fern Velocity

Whatever their thoughts are drip into the ground
Chinese takeout
      in compostable bags
            High arches
                  Green insoles
                  Prescriptions pushing up
            through capillaries
      & eviction notices
Making an initial
descent into nonstop mist & early forest smells

They sign everything electronically even seasons
Green fruit leather
      after rain
            Silent in sunlight they
                  chatter in shade down the days
                  Familybrained &
            hitched to one thought
      Every other tooth
a twin
Traffic lights bounce back those same nerve endings

Bits of steak from flossing teeth burn off in the bark dust
Folding chairs
    beneath that one ceaseless bird
        On airplane mode
            species hearing
            hears atmosphere as footsteps
        Teeth give out
    at the edge of what is that
a whistle in a hedge
Prettyprettyprettyprettyprettyprettyprettyprettypretty

Lift beats drag at knee level & shakes the cabin out
Everyone talks
        at the same time
                They hear dog frequency
                        leafed out
                        in rolling frond breakers
                A repeating cyst
        buttoned down the back
Muck out their own eggs
Return their seat trays to an upright position & sleep

Sudden relief the color of stadium light in 7UP bottles
A green tape recorder
    commits everything to the ground
        No more frozen peas
            No more conference calls
            Cell commotion
        in the duff
    Baseball diamonds from above
Spring couplets
between takeoff & landing the overhead lights switch off

The Poem Said

The poem said
that sunlight back there is the only thing
I like
Pour it back into starter beds or leave it on the sill for neighbors or for
later
A grassy smell in the kitchen

Lidocaine floats
the fringed tulips in a crease & that's the morning
There's so much to look forward to
Big bowls of cereal
A tonal shift in the fertilizer

Later automatic ramen & a Coke
You can start anywhere it doesn't really matter
Flowers on the table
breathe sugar
The skylight in the dosage doesn't

Wildstyle

Aerosol flower in the middle of the air
makes one perfect
what

butterfly / buttercup
their open faces
the color of yellow street signs
Most flowers I love more than people
but who cares
about people?

Your technique leaves me weak

Foamflowers
& milkdrops against
a green screen of ferns

& just last Saturday my baby daughter was born

Her mouth is a dish of milk

Oh they're
snowdrops

ROSE PARADE

Tea Roses

Extra light
licks the edges off a hot one
today is sprayed on
pink-pink
pealed & spastic

They smell like food
wrapped around a single thought

Getting married
upon reentry into the earth's
starter beds
Pink starts
Pink air made out of gas giants
Floating on their backs in a chromosome wash surrounded by fragrance
  experts

Honore de Balzac & Marilyn Monroe
hold hands
a child's voice can't
get this pink

Fertilizer

Let's replace the dog run with test roses
I said to Mom
through her cigarette

More weeding
Less dogs

Leaves are layered & zipped up in full racing leathers have you noticed?
The moon too
& Mom's smile
mostly I came up here in high school
A rose parade
right now in the kitchen
is beautiful
& always will be

The dogs race down an aisle or two

The fluttery red ones
we did not
grow them ourselves

Test Roses

Apparently you separate the whites
& such petals in the palm
then a Coke or two & some sunlight on the grass
My aunt Dot said bonemeal
put bonemeal in
The small yellow ones
I didn't get a chance to yet but the greenhouse does the same
Aphids type their names
just like you or me
on water

Through bud bursts
turning leaves into text messages
with their teeth

Live from the garden its small faces look up at us
in powdered rows

Paper Cups

All in a line
but with the sound off
sepals curl away from some other
beginning

Tight green stacks

The pink red orange & yellow ones were a kind of VistaVision
scrolled above the known
grass & dog shit

Try to grow something you don't understand

Sugar & fertilizer or
white moss

Tent loopers or leaf rollers
call from another
nibble

An entire culture

I look up from what I am doing in sunglasses

Rose City

Turbulence in the filament or a leaflet
with your address on it
The buses are running
over the Morrison & up Salmon
Salmon scales & species shyness
in compost & high heels
A queen is still a queen
Post-royal hangups the new branding campaigns were geared toward
sunsets & picnics
In the International Rose Test Garden
they breathe all at once
Leaves coated in powder-blue insect shit
a public service
See-through white petals the color of Noh drama
Everything is below
the Japanese gardens
A vascular system inhales wet signals
turn the corner & you're there

A friend flicks alive a pink Bic

Not a rose
but a clove cigarette

LRS

Lakes Rivers Streams

Fish tap tap tap on the roof

Water rushes by through the living room into the kitchen late night &

look someone thought to load the dishwasher

A lamp is on in the other room

Two lamps

Lampreys swirl in a bucket from last night's dream

I had wanted to dream about birds & all I got were these

eels

Who could I call to ask what to do?

Who might move the peonies back into the kitchen who might

change their water?

Other things get started

Peepers

Stuck in jelly

At the same time spring pushes up against the windows

a green crease

& sleep

Pooled at the top of the stairs

Who could I call to make an appointment

or swim?

Cows float in the bunch

Scraps of brown paper

I learn to swim in the afternoon with everyone else my age

A sale of Holsteins & Herefords

You can smell the detergent in the yard with

the other flowers

When I woke up this morning the lights were already on in the clover

Hunkered down on all fours to see it maybe press your nose

against it

Like rabbits

The bottoms of her baby feet

My son's hair is still gold & smells like wheat

The porch light sluiced through the patch grass so we might know

where we were or were not

At home or away

Just upstream from a cell tower & a box of Huggies

Who would dabble the backyard & who flush out

those rabbits?

The neighbors are already at it

Just upstream from a can of Red Bull & a pollen allergy

The old mower used gasoline but this new one you just plug into a wall

Trim the edges

An orange extension cord crawls out from the dining room

into the sun

The entire afternoon stacked up on the edge of

the patio

Dandelions with their heads chopped off & my mother's one or other

dog or is that a deer?

Deer file up to the window to look at you

A gardening problem in the suburbs

Deer pellets

Your little fingers opening an apple opening

a star

Feeding it to a deer

The seeds inside were red watermelon seeds

A light sweat breaks out over the milk carton

Not only that but also fish piled in the back of a truck or slung into

waxed bags

A silver leak

Where is everyone?

My kids slide inside their wet rooms asleep

A bag of Chinook a bag of

Silverside?

Leaking onto a pile of ferns

A light wash overflows this regular morning

Aspirin with codeine is nice & something to look forward to outside

    of a blank slate

The cool floors of grocery stores

The side of your cheek in the morning

    a fish cheek

Safeway is open ditto Fred Meyer's

The fridge opens by itself & leaks something almost lettuce almost

    milk

Just upstream from a pair of headphones & a Weight Watchers

Not only a light on in the refrigerator but a puddle lit from inside

A dragonfly drags through grass

        & trash

You don't get to be the grass

That dragonfly probly isn't even a dragonfly probly it's a deerfly

Snapdragons!

I dreamt we started the whole day over from scratch

Poured that out onto the floor

Not only static in the trees when I wake but something whipped up

    into glossy foam

Chirrup-chirrup my tree makes syrup

    syrup so sweet

Just upstream from a can of Aqua Net & a Pepsi

Metallic twist ties

Just opened this morning

Skipping down the grandmother sidewalk without stepping on a crack

No one to catch it or hold it

No one to pull the light out of the rhododendrons by hand with their

        own hands

Mom calls from the dog run in the backyard

A minor threat

A dog floats by another dog

Put the coffee on I'll be right in!

Wind from I-5 kicks up her green jogger & a pretty seamless

        dye job

Stuck in a tree

No one to clean out the freezer gas the car or even

take a message

The eels are both boys & girls all at once

They swim under the couch & disappear

The sun goes on despite disappointing coverage

& lower fees

Mom does her hair

What would you like to do with this pile of cellphones?

What would you like to eat?

The baby likes dogs & flowers

Bees in the lilac have something to say & say it without giving

        away the ending

A yellow retriever mix or black Lab or roses

Royal Gold or Ruby Ruby

That lilac probly isn't even a lilac probly it's a wisteria

Press PLAY

Her little fingers can't yet work

        a button

Not only a list of ants making its way from a crack in the concrete to a

scrap in the sink

Flower Carpet Coral or Flower Carpet Pink

But milk in the ground

Babymeal

Something opens in the day & you

step right through

The ants are interesting they stick together all in a line or a ring

circling

The rings of Saturn

Oh look someone thought to pick up the tennis balls & miscellaneous toys

before plugging in the mower

Or a spaniel or a boxer

No one to pick her up or hold her?

Blight was a word we never used as the roses took or

they didn't

The baby?

Fragrant Cloud Fragrant Plum

The grass is tennis-ball green

But also that deerfly could have been a mosquito just outside the

    service area

I could finally get through to you to reach you!

The tips of its fingers

Paper or plastic?

If you want birds you might try a bird feeder

Just upstream from a gallon of 2% & a yellow pack of American Spirits

Stick on your mosquito body or yellow swimsuit

    & swim

But also the kids breathing inside their mammal rooms breathing

    water

Someone left the bougainvillea on all night ditto the humidifier

Same frequency as the rhoddy's

You could hear it for a long time after

Their dream names Sharpied onto the side of a white

    plastic bag

I could finally do that

No one has called my cellphone now for hours

Cherry blossoms call to the surface of things that is

        their color

In contrast to almost everything else on the floor

My dream kids shit in buckets

Frogs try to get on them

Who will shoe their pretty little feet who will hold their hands?

This is the earth & sometimes the earth

        changes color

Now I remember they were horses mulching the backyard

Who will polish their shiny little shoes?

Who will pick them flowers?

A regular morning

You nuzzle open a pile of cherries & there it was the thing we

always wanted

Whatever that was

A chain-link fence goes round & round

like a song

They sleep standing in a circle

Dandelions pee in a corner of the yard a kind of Kodak yellow

Lamb's-tongue ditto the coltsfoot

My horse kids eat something off the ground I can't quite make out

        some leather fruits & Oh's

Nosing in the dark

Nosing inside holes

Lay their necks across my

        one neck

Just upstream from a microwave & a tub of Cool Whip

Noses against the sliding glass door squeak a little at night that is

their sound

Noses against visitors

Who will mow around their calves?

Mom said she wasn't sure

Not one memory of a butterfly back there but horseflies somehow in

the neighbor grass

Eat the roses

Dig a little hole & get into it

What should I do with their withers & fetlocks what should I do with

    their dressage?

A parade is nice

I shoveled the backyard for a picnic but you could still smell it

The tomatoes almost took ditto

    the basil

Not only today but also tomorrow

Noses in the dark

Manure noses

The day curled up in a cup

A private life you can hear above the washer or was that the mower

even now it's two blocks away

Listening is yellow & green

Coho swim in cellphones

Speakers set up thoughtfully throughout the house did you

notice that?

Skin wings on the back of another animal or person

Eating out a radio

The day curled up in a corner

Butterfly flutter harder to hear the closer you are to the window

isn't that odd?

Skateboards on the macadam

Switch Heel & Kickflip via a Frontside 180

I couldn't see the kids before they were born though they threw

their voices

An earful of leaf blowers

Then they were here

The day was moving off somewhere

    hard to see

The day was both

At first I thought I could hear them through leaves & understory but

    then I wasn't so sure

Curled up on the couch

You both do & you don't

More a davenport than anything else

Just upstream from a can of Lemon Pledge & a pack of Gorton's

Did I tell you I watered the cherry tree in the backyard ditto

    the crape myrtle?

Is that what's it called?

Talking to maple leaves makes for a nice morning if quiet

    at first & then loud

Day moves toward the door

A box fan instead of air-conditioning

I can't tell their voices apart

Across the articulated lawn something glows is that a glass of milk?

Kids curled up on the coating

An earwig floats by another earwig

The day listens to traffic moving off in two directions at once like

standing in a spring shower

Flowers appear without warning

& whom do we have to thank for this delicious lunch?

These petits fours?

That one & only

glass of milk?

For instance you walk through the room without

        looking up

The door opens out onto a new paint job & makes for a pleasant surprise

Light a cigarette in there

Those Chinook & Silverside probly aren't probly they're rainbow

        trout & organic salmon

A spoonful of roe

No place to light your fingers

Or move them back & forth

For instance the phone keeps ringing in the other room

Beneath a tea cozy

Just upstream from a toilet cover &

a Percocet

More a lilac than anything else

An ant floats by another ant

A lucid upwelling

But you don't even know how to have fun anymore you don't even like

to do drugs

Sidewalks glint in sun & trees newly opened oh shit I woke up with a

tension headache!

Pear blossoms

They smell like semen

For instance I look forward to seeing you all day

No place to put our feet up or

say anything

Blah blah blahblahblah

Quick let's do it before the kids wake up!

ıorning before

ıeal

‹ind of life because we had

ℓ slow

More a migraine than anything else

Something dull in the bushes is that a rabbit?

A dead squirrel whirligigs

        the light

That light was ClingFree

For instance a Coke is nice & something to look forward to & you

        can do it by yourself

The day knows exactly what it's doing

Opening a stuck window or collecting a small fee

But also you see something out the window I don't see

Moss grows you can count on it

Morning dew scratches at the door then canters away into what we're

not sure of

I filtered everything through rain & got what exactly

more rain?

The good news is ferns

The good news is graffiti

Those peonies probly weren't even peonies probly they're dahlias

But also the kids pick flowers if you let them

Some petals are soapy & blow down the street a quick & linty pink

    & white dream

As for TV there's always perennials

As for daycare there's always the grass

A pile of nachos in the microwave

Just upstream from a car battery & a glass of SunnyD

Benadryl in the grass & grass insects tuning up the tardy afternoon

    a twitchy kickstart

Her sneeze in the puffed-out dandelions his little cough someplace else

altogether

It's time for lunch

It's time for the sun

Just because you carry something from one day to the next it doesn't

make all days the same

Everybody out of the pool!

The skimmers are brightly colored & constant

The skimmers are chlorined & cousined

Not only recycling but holding hands in a holding pattern the day

spends outside

Tied up with kitchen twine & stacked neatly by the curb

A cardboard floats by another cardboard

The next thing you know the rain has stopped

& starts again before you know it kicking over blossoms &

sidewalk trash

A cup of coffee on the counter

The dogs in the backyard in a lather

Just upstream from a VHS player & a bucket of KFC

Stars look down & count the tops

    of our heads

A cellphone tower via a pine tree

The newly emptied mall parking lot via a lake

I got here late

Wildstyle via Fat Cap along the chain link was red & yellow spray roses

The top of my daughter's head ditto the top

    of my son's

The afternoon leans toward television & birds

A dream can stay on all morning hanging around for drop-off &

early pickup

Just in time for a quick once-over

The pansies took ditto the ground cover

More an annual than anything else

The top of my daughter's head is astro fluff in the

atmosphere

Blue jays on shuffle in the electronic trees

For instance bees make their home in the sandbox

The sound of the interstate via the sound of

the sea

Margarine via butter

The top of my son's head is corn silk shot through a cassette deck

playing early Black Flag

Alone in the kitchen

Mom presses REWIND on the microwave

Dogs melt in linoleum

Not only that but you don't have to feel bad anymore

Blue jay by blue jay

The birds are real & wait just outside an open signal or

a Pingo

Just upstream from the new mixed-use building concern & a

two-liter of Diet Squirt

Wings in the wallpaper

Wings & glue

I wasn't going to do it again but maybe you could describe

the light?

It's not easy but it's a little

easier

Probly those earwigs weren't even earwigs probly they were roly-polys

Our loved ones are everywhere

Leaves buffeted by the HVAC system

Their names whispered through an intercom in the evergreens

The blue jay's nesting material was modern & shining recyclables

reflected off the surface of the lawn

A twist of tinfoil in the shape of a swan

A cloud of dryer lint soundproofs the scrape

Open wires braided in a fishtail braid or a 6-pack yoke in a

classic milkmaid

Cotton wool jute & burlap

Feathers from other birds mixed with uncoated paper

& fiberglass

Just upstream from a bottle of Sumatriptan & a case of bottled water

More a grocery list than anything else

A single zigzag

Tinsel blings the classic cup

Leaves repurposed as sanitizer & a kind of traditional blockwood

painted or flocked wallpaper

Banana leaves & artichokes on fast-forward

Cellulose is waterproof

Human hair or horschair in a starburst carousel

Not only plastic strips but cellophane draped over the vegetation

A crown calls from a cornrow

A titmouse calls from a saucer or plate

A wire hanger bends this regular afternoon into a dressing chair

without a seating assignment

Dead twigs dead leaves & dry

grass

Reclaimed corners

Reclaimed grass

That monoprint of a maple leaf on the platform

A phosphorous updo

For instance neighbor kids find a nest & check on it each morning

balanced on a pile of chairs

The ground looks up & then returns to whatever it was doing before

Curbside check-in for squeakers

Curbside check-in for suet

Broom bristles mop string &

dental floss

An onion bag in a topknot

A twist of tinfoil in the shape of a Park-n-Ride

For instance a light applause breaks out over the swing-set slide &

seesaw combo

Did I tell you I aced the bathroom?

A roll of toilet paper

Scotch-Brite & a butter knife

Probly that nest wasn't even a nest probly it was a custom

four-in-hand

Warm water white vinegar & Arm & Hammer

An upload of sunlight

For instance butterflies have tongues & hang them out in the day to

pick up what exactly?

The local station we used to get we don't get anymore

Voicemail via an otter

A block graph via a bluebell

Their tongues curl in the light of a flat-screen projecting a host plant

& a finale

Four long two short

Sip-sipping a hotspot

For instance the grass looks up & then goes back to whatever

it was doing before

A very heavy rain followed by a very light rain

Did I tell you I replaced everything &

all at once?

Dog shit in the backyard

The day in a V shape planted in parks parkways & yards or

seasonally planted around the house

An attachment via an acorn

A chat room via a catkin

If the day is fernlike & pointed at the ends & irregular or keeled as

the times & styles change

A four-ring box clutch via a pillbox

A glass organza via a clinkerbell

Those blue jays probly weren't even blue jays probly they were

finches

You can't put the day back together again

A decal of a hawk silhouette

Just upstream from a pair of headphones & a Stouffer's

If the day is tapered leaf stems with a white undersurface tolerating

the usual errands

A tree in the shade of a tree

An ozone inside a loophole

More a Lean Cuisine than anything else

We let the grass go yellow on purpose & drove straight

to the store

My daughter pulls the grass up with her fingers

My son uses scissors

If the day is deciduous & thin with waves at the margins &

common or common enough

Did I tell you I vacuumed the carpets & dusted

the picture window?

A picture of what?

An airplane in the shape of the Willamette

Meanwhile the river looks up & then goes back to whatever it was

doing before

A landing strip via some riprap

Our futures in a bindle

If the day is untidy-looking & aromatic with end leaflets narrowing

where the sun is lopsided & lobed

We can't leave the kids in the car anymore

Or wind or cows or people

I'll wait outside

Schist in your shoes picks up where we left off

A photo offset of a fern into a

spreadsheet

A blue flame in the new gas stove

If the day is irregular on both sides & pebbled or modified by acrylics

& permanent

Black toner cartridge via a starling

A stop bath via a sparrow

The afternoon clears the table for flowers & more

television

Not only whatever's on but a pinnate in the past

More a dinette set than anything else

The day ticking over in the fixer bath

Meanwhile a northern flicker bends a piece of Plexiglas into a wind

chime

Did I tell you I raked the leaves & put them all back into a black

Glad bag?

Meanwhile a black-capped chickadee

One kid asleep upstairs another on the pot

Bird clutter marks the spot

Just upstream from a newly relaxed regulation & the brand-new

Jiffy Lube

A birdbath in a dribble

A damselfly vacates the day in a blur

A mosquito on a daisy

My daughter looks up & then goes back to whatever it was she was

doing before

The afternoon divided up into zones

Where her new sounds meanwhile astound the daylight

on a leaf

An off-brand beetle duct tapes the water

X's & O's

You don't have to if you don't want to

Pink rollers via a ripple

Little white sticks via a balk

Meanwhile a deer tick slides into the very last reserved parking spot

Under arms around the ears back of the knees &

        between the legs

Meanwhile inside a belly button

A pink parking pass swivels between the seat cushions

A speckle-winged quill vacates the day in a blind

More a swidge than anything else

That grass probly wasn't even grass probly it was a roll of Diamond

        Pro Fescue or Jade 50

A blue tint ditto a cloud of flies

Meanwhile a water strider enamels the edge of a pond making

        room for the rest of the day

A stork inside your mind

Dots & lines

In other places we felt much the same as we do today only

more so

Meanwhile a mayfly floats by another mayfly

A hard drive via a hedge

A Bluetooth via a squiggle

Oh look someone remembered to take out the compost

Meanwhile mites in a double clasp & peaked felt number wish you

well & more

White foam scours a polished floor

Who will tape their wings back?

Who will fold their corners?

A common green lacewing has an appointment someplace else

    altogether & will keep it

To a thrip or a honeydew

A grand tour

Just upstream from a stackable washer/dryer unit & the brand-new

    FreshDirect

Pellets perk up the leaf litter

Before you know it that light has changed from checker mallow &

milkweed to something more en suite

Whites & sulphurs

Probly that lacewing wasn't even a lacewing probly it was a green

smudge

Hey! Hey kids!

Meanwhile a green comma or a common

ringlet

Their wings are made of cardboard & Reynolds Wrap

A rubber band here a rubber band there

Meanwhile real sunlight sneaks up the wall somewhere between

    butterfly yellow & butterfly brown

Not a dream really just an ordinary afternoon

What color is that goldenrod?

A focal point via a knob

The new streaming service was all aflutter & temporarily

    unavailable

Not only that but a golden hairstreak

One kid on the couch the other in a bole

Just between the dimmer switch & a short circuit of local or overlit

Western lilies

Hi-Liter yellow & chisel-tipped

A bucket of honeysuckle

Bring the car around I'll be right out!

Did I tell you I aced the console with some Orange Glo ditto the late

afternoon?

They blanket the lawn in summer

A long dash followed by a short dash

Right between a commotion of track lighting & a dribble of newish

antibiotics

A newish drop in the bucket

An overflow of stillness & snacks

My son looks up & then goes back to whatever it was he was

doing before

The day is nonslip & early

A download of nervy & rainbowed fluorescence

A bedhead floats by another bedhead

Just between the newly installed porch floods & a small handful of

cabbage whites

A vertical frequency to it

A sprinkle of what exactly?

Not only that but our intentions stacked

in a swirl

The bunting's vocals were lip-synced & weird ditto the dishwasher's

A voice box via a gorge

A yellow Lego via a suncup

Right between a semi-transparent aftereffect & a latticed or

crosshatched bit of fluff

An upgrade via a wrinkle

More a floater than anything else

Probly that bunting wasn't even a bunting probly it was a Western

Wood-Peewee

We began with sliced apple & later moved on to sunlight

An orange tip on a pincushion

A pip on the carpet

Or an inverted firefly blinking on & off through a drift of dandruff

flicked off the TV set

A flittery cat's-eye

Yellow green or pale red

Just upstream from a can of Sea Foam & a bag of Birds Eye single

steamers

An additive combination of bark dust &

grade school

Or a premium glow stick

The tops of trees

Or an elliptical wastebasket where my son might pick out a glowworm

        or a lime-green flashlight fish

The day has its limits

The yard looks the same now than it did just an hour ago

Same rush of Oregon grape same hurry of

        salmonberry

The names for things slip away

A rotary via a spiral

A router via a tangle

Or a streamer bobs its way across the living room trailing a yellow

    popper through the topwater

My daughter ties off an improved clinch knot

A perfection loop

The day is construction paper

    & laundry

It syrups the corners

Not only that but the remote control scuddled in the wingback

Wide-open spaces

Or a glint off the kitchen counter where a local slope wrinkles a bowl

    of cereal on the new Formica

The toaster shimmies

A splake floats by another splake

Did I tell you I folded the clothes in a basic reverse squash or rabbit

    fold ditto the onesies?

The day is sound checked &

    perennial

Appearing & disappearing in the hydrangeas

A plus sign followed by a minus

Or a speck of something else altogether some mica or something made

of OJ bits & squinting

A dreamy dusky wing

Meanwhile the grass is back

Butter & eggs are seamless & window box the stand mixer organic

dish soap & phone

A private suburb here where we put things

A plug-in via a stob

Rods & cones

Or cuckoo bees spun out in a bright wash of parallel & early or late

climber roses

Just upstream from a buffet-style weekend special & some notable

losses

Pollen paints the car & cleans out eczema

Wicks out the margins

Wisteria points up the positives of nonverbal

choral work

Or music you can't hear

Water music

Or a flowering piggyback petals a residue of light-to-dark jellies &

purple glue stuff

A smidgen of Windex

A gimlet in waves

Probly that cat's-eye wasn't even a cat's-eye probly it was a clinky

toothpaste

At the same time heaps of clouds bounce off

the driveway

I plated the snacks ditto the expectations

Burnt toast & bitumen

Or outside the voices of other children climb up

Taller ones

Pedal bikes push up & down the walk all day transfigure the

pavements in a wired curlicue

A fiddlehead with arms & legs

Or taller trees in a chase

The day is non-glare & leafed out stuccoed by

robot beetles

One television is off the other is vertical rays of light

Or a #2 pencil beam crinkles the cornea in the backyard feathering

seed starters & stems

The day feels irreversible & will stay inside a Dixie cup

Things stick to the door screen

Windy light broken off & moth dust broken off

Ribs & holes

Not only that but a complicated system of noticing & a dob of

apple juice

You blow on it & it glows

Or a refurbished working day backlights the hanging geraniums a

handful of pink fiberglass

A lake effect glancing off the sideboard

A streamer via a stickle

A cooler via a brook

More than that those green & gold flecked inlays look away

A creek bed in the hallway

A spiral floats by another spiral

& pink and blue transparencies gel the day each morning

& pansies more than you

You don't have to wonder about the sky anymore you don't have to ask

what to wear

Just upstream from a sketchy weather system & the new overpass

High on glue

The raindrops can't lash the ferns they can't

flashflood a pinna

Then the sun comes out again

& trees are stressed out & can't get going either

It's dinnertime breakfast is over

Over & over my son's voice across the lawn a white sparkler then a

green sparkler then a white

Someone comes running

Probly those geraniums aren't even geraniums probly they're

trailing accents

Local traffic

Left to your own devices you would watch TV clips all day & make

more toast & then what brush your teeth?

& vacuuming the carpet makes a nice smell part burnt tips part

            wet dog

It's difficult to think of something to do

A snip floats by another snip

I guess what you're doing today is doing chores

I picked up everything in the house & set it all back down just to

            the left of the clicker

Pajamas & urine

A throw rug via a jelly roll

& it's color time & petal time & leaves lift the light outside

  the window just enough

I let the flowers back in ditto the dog

You only have a few minutes for anything it's hardly enough time

  to get started

Hey! Hey trees!

Did I tell you I scoured the linoleum with an X-Acto & cleaned out

  the wayback?

One tree is pine & one is maple I know that

One tree is on its way

& a handheld Japanese coffee grinder collects dust & would after

any wedding not just ours

Bags of groceries wait in a brown line

A skater floats by another skater

Green feedback

Golden raisins

If you want to hear lake water lapping their thousand tongues pushing

past duckweed you'll have to imagine it

A basin inside a teacup

Where slices of orange radiate a Ziploc

No one uses sprinklers here except the university we're just as happy

with people

Just upstream from your first home & anything that's left over

Repetitions in crinoline

Local neon

If you want to hear the lawn service line up edges in sunlight you'll

have to wait until Wednesday

In the morning the kids come running down the stairs

ACKNOWLEDGMENTS

Grateful acknowledgment is due to Paul Muldoon and Kevin Young at *The New Yorker* for publishing "Hotel Days" and "The Poem Said (that sunlight back there . . .)," to Ahern Warner at *Poetry London* for publishing "Butterfly Days," and to Don Share at *POETRY* magazine, where "Lakes Rivers Streams" first appeared.

*

The title "The Poem Said" is Franz Wright's.

*

"Butterfly Days" is for Maureen N. McLane.
"Hotel Days" is for Karen Solie.

*

"Rose Parade" is for Thomas Lauderdale.

A NOTE ABOUT THE AUTHOR

Michael Dickman was born and
raised in the Pacific Northwest.

A NOTE ON THE TYPE

The text of this book was set in Sabon, a typeface designed by Jan Tschichold (1902–1974).

Designed and typeset by Michael Collica

Printed and bound by Thomson-Shore
Dexter, Michigan